Ask New Questions
Get Better Results

LAURA BERMAN FORTGANG

DEDICATION

To all the wonderful clients and students
who have endured my questions

CONTENTS

ACKNOWLEDGMENTS

Joel Fotinos is the force behind this little book. He saw an opportunity for me and he assigned it to me to expedite.

I thank you, Joel. Not only for the little push, but also for caring enough to suggest it. It was a great idea to take one of my big teaching points and make it a work of its own. Everyone should have a friend like you.

PROLOGUE

There are times when something you once thought was a negative matures into an unexpected and welcomed outcome. Have you ever been grateful for a bad experience in hindsight? I have a fistful of stories of that ilk, and I bet you do, too. The one I want to share explains how this book on questions found its origin. It's the reason these tools you're about to discover came to be.

In the first five years of my coaching career, I never went without my own coach. (Now, I hire a coach annually, but not consistently.) One of the coaches I worked with early on was not as good a fit for me as I initially thought. Once I could put my finger on what was causing me to feel uneasy, I realized it had to do with the questions the coach asked me during the course of our sessions.

It dawned on me one day after a particularly frustrating session that all the questions this coach was asking me seemed to be for his edification and not for my benefit. I wasn't moving forward. I wasn't making changes. I was reporting news, details and information, and each session left me feeling antsy and wrung out.

From that hiccup, I saw a powerful way to transform my own coaching. While questions had always been part of how I did what I did, I suddenly had the understanding of what made an effective question and what did not.

I've used the techniques you're about to read about for years in my professional and personal life. I've taught them to thousands of coaches, and I devoted a chapter to them in one of my earlier books, *Living Your Best Life*. I've shared them in companies large and small – in speeches to large groups and in trainings in small rooms.

You are getting my best thinking fourteen years AFTER writing that chapter, so what awaits you is updated and even easier to digest.

A negative transformed into a positive brings you this book. I am grateful for the discovery of the distinctions in question asking that my negative experience showed me. What an amazing WIN it ended up being!

I hope you find the reading of this book a positive experience and that it helps you to create many wins in your life. I have no doubt you'll turn many a difficult conversation or encounter into an easier, more positive one once you get the hang of it.

Laura Berman Fortgang
New Jersey, September 11, 2014

CHAPTER ONE
WHY QUESTIONS MATTER

What do you want? Answers? Better solutions? Relief from suffering? To be able to help a friend with a problem? Or maybe you'd just like to find it easier to meet strangers or make conversation at parties or business meetings.

Questions are the answer.

Asking better questions will get you better results. They could even make you happy because they have the potential to improve your mood and physiology. (Did you know that?) The right kinds of questions can put you into forward motion and dig you out of problems. This tweak in language can result in you becoming unstuck, lightening your mood and improving mental clarity and focus. That's an "I'll have what she/he's-having" scenario if I've ever heard one!

The right questions can take you out of an unproductive line of thinking. They can release you if you've gotten emotionally hooked – caught in an endless loop obsessively playing in your head.

The methods are not difficult, but they are probably new to you. It's not how we are taught to communicate with ourselves or with others. It may feel unnatural at first, but in time, you won't ask questions any other way.

It's probably only fair to warn you that mastering what you are about to learn herein could garner you some push-back from the people in your life. If you don't warn them of your new questioning prowess, you may suddenly appear very direct and somewhat confrontational to them if you are not already like that. The questions you are going to learn about shortly will make it hard for people to keep up what are usually innocuous social fibs. I've had people in my personal life hang up their phone on me when I've gone into question-asking mode out of habit, forgetting that I've likely stepped over the line of most people's comfort zone.

I'm not telling you this to scare you before we even get started, but, rather, to let you know you'll be absorbing some powerful tools that not everyone is ready for. You may need to tread lightly at first until you get used to wielding such a big, powerful sword. Ultimately, no one will get hurt, but being on the spot isn't everyone's preferred place to hang out.

You've been cautioned. Don't let that stop you.

Whether you're wishing you could find answers to your own life queries, be a better conversationalist, deal with interpersonal issues better in your office or among family, or just be a sharper communicator, learning the questions put forth in this book will help with in ways you may not have thought of yet.

Questions can become new tools for a better life.

CHAPTER TWO
DO YOU WANT PROBLEMS
OR SOLUTIONS?

We are both smart enough to know that
you would not purposely choose to have
problems, but it may just be that you are not
aware of how you seek them out. That's not
to say any problems you do have are your
fault or that you asked for them, but many of
us are wired to see the problem instead of the
solution.

You may be a recovering perfectionist or
self-identified as a master problem solver,
therefore seeking more problems to solve.
Your job or identity as a problem-solver may
be working very well for you. However, being
entwined with problems as the core of your
success may have shaped you to become very

problem-oriented and perhaps helpless to
solve issues for yourself.

If you want to train yourself to ask
questions that yield solutions and forward
motion, you are first going to have to shift
your modus operandi from problem-
orientation to solution-orientation. People
who solve problems tend to ask questions to
gather information and assess a situation.
They go on a fact-finding mission, absorbing
every detail, ultimately allowing them to assess
and fix. That can be a talent in itself, but if
your life isn't going the way you'd like, an
understanding of whether or not you process
in a problem-focused way could help you gain
new perspective.

People who are focused on moving
forward and painting a picture of a new
direction or possibility ask questions like an

artist adds brushstrokes to a canvas — adding to the big picture through discovery and creating as they go.

Look at the characteristics described below. Each column describes a different intention behind asking questions. Which one best describes you?

Are You A Problem-Seeker?

- Asks questions that are self-centered (What's wrong with me, the world, the situation in relation to how it affects me?)

- Digs for evidence to justify point of view

- Is oriented toward solving problems

- Gives answers as part of identity

- Is territorial and assumes everything is scarce

- Sees knowledge as a source of power

- Hoards and controls information

- Reacts without thinking

Are You A Solution-Seeker?

- Asks questions that are focused outward
  (What's right about me, the world, the situation?)

- Is oriented toward solutions

- Sees knowledge as a source of power to be shared

- Assumes ample resources are available

- Acts as objective observer to find truth

- Uses information is used to inspire and transform

- Thinks and reflects before taking action or speaking

- Is comfortable with waiting for answers

- Is OK appearing to "not know" temporarily

Each list will give you choices as to how you use questions and help you determine which characteristics you are predisposed to.

There is nothing wrong with finding yourself in the problem-seeker list, but you will see that you could be making better choices, asking different questions and producing less stressful outcomes if you focus on becoming the solution-seeker.

The solution-seeker is the creator of a new future. The problem-seeker is a fixer of the past. The problem-seeker/fixer could accomplish the task and come up with a solution, however the solution-seeker may see beyond the problem to something that can sustain success and change much longer with a more productive outcome.

Traveling around the United States this last year, I had the opportunity to brainstorm and be with CEOs of small businesses ($4 million to $100 million). It was fascinating to see how so many of them were strongly identified with being problem-fixers. They looked for problems and solved them to great satisfaction. Few of them were likely to look further out into the future to create solutions that did not require them to be present to solve what came up. Few were willing to make themselves less critical to the operation to have solutions that could outlast their presence in the problem-solving puzzle.

If they could make this critical change, they'd have the potential to create smoother operational horizons. For many of them, the identity as problem-seeker/problem-fixer was precious to them. They see their fixer prowess as an intrinsic part of their identity. They'd be afraid to be rendered useless if they were to consider giving up that identity.

This brings me to an interesting phenomenon I've seen in my coaching work for decades. I've come to call this curiosity the "Hero Syndrome." This is my pet name for an unconscious or semi-conscious tendency I see in many people to save the day and be the hero even at the expense of their own sanity.

The Hero Syndrome is when someone falls into an addictive loop of being the hero in situations. It doesn't discriminate. It's not a problem only leaders have. Anyone that can save the day and be the one everyone depends on for answers or action can fall prey to the habit. Being the one trusted with private information and many other 'adventures' that raise our adrenaline makes us feel needed and integral to the process. This keeps us hooked in an endless loop of giving that starts to diminish our ability to do our own jobs sometimes and pursue our own dreams and desires.

I once worked with a senior vice president of sales in a large pharmaceutical company who was in a particular time of busyness and turmoil when we began working together. She knew things had become unmanageable, but she couldn't decipher what was the root cause of the chaos. She kept complaining that she spent her days putting out fires and being pulled in many directions while constantly being distracted from her own deliverables.

She didn't boast, but I could tell there was a certain amount of satisfaction in being needed so much and being the one with the answers. However, I knew I wouldn't be doing her the greatest service by helping her do the juggling act better. Instead, I finally got her to answer a better question. I asked: "What is the source of the fires?"

She answered that the department she kept getting pulled into had no leadership of their own. She admitted that the job at hand was to support them in identifying a leader and to stop solving all their problems.

Now let's see if you are a "HERO." Take the quiz below.

Are You Suffering from the Hero Syndrome?

Undoubtedly, we are a culture of people who do too much. Whether you're a professional or a domestic demi-god, you may be paying dearly for it in your effectiveness, satisfaction, well-being, quality of life, or family and personal time. In fact, you may be suffering from The Hero Syndrome.

Check the statements below that are true for you. Be brutally honest. If an item causes a strong reaction because you don't want it to be true, you can bet it's true for you.

1. I'm often the one on whom people depend in a pinch.

2. I'm someone whom several people trust with private information.

3. I'm often overwhelmed by the obligations I have to meet because of promises I've made to others.

4. It's important for me to feel needed.

5. I get great satisfaction from knowing that I'm the only one who can solve a specific problem.

6. It's hard for me to delegate tasks.

7. I have several friends or colleagues who only call me when they need something.

8. I usually volunteer for a task or project.

9. It's difficult for me to receive praise even when I deserve it.

10. I want to feel calm and in control more often.

11. It's hard for me to end each day with a sense of accomplishment because there's always so much more to do.

12. I'm the first one to begin my day at work or at home and the last one to call it quits.

13. I catch myself complaining about the same problems over and over again.

14. I often count on adrenaline to get through the day.

15. I'm not compensated with money, rewards, or recognition for the extra things I take on.

SCORING

Give yourself one point for each statement that you marked true. Then look below to see where you stand.

0 - 2   Congratulations! You set your limits and honor your own priorities and well-being

3 - 5   You are predisposed to The Hero Syndrome. Work to keep things in check now so that you don't pay the price later.

6 - 10   You make life harder than it needs to be. Start setting boundaries and giving back responsibility to others.

11 - 15 You're suffering from The Hero Syndrome. Without a doubt, you're exhausted and have little room to enjoy work or life. Take immediate and radical action to reverse this condition

If you scored on the higher side of the quiz, you can see where your tendency to be a problem-seeker comes from. If you want a higher quality of life and/or a greater leadership role and recognition at work, it's time to quit this habit.

If you're at the top of the food chain in an organizational chart, the future of your business depends on you being dispensable. You have to quit being the hero too. Your task is to become the creator of a new future and stop being the frontlines warrior of the problems in your space. It's like becoming the queen bee instead of the worker-bee in your own life.

Create for a larger vision – the vision of the hive, not just the vision of the limited flower-to flower existence of the worker bee.

How do you shed this identity and stop needing its delusional rewards? Change your questions.

If you're ready to leave problems behind and become a solution-seeker, the next chapter will show you how to temper your mindset in order to start moving into asking the questions that will get you better results.

CHAPTER THREE
DON'T SOLVE – ASK!

If you'd like to reduce stress, get the people you work with to be more independent of you, have your family members consider you the wise one, and guide other people to solve their own problems, you'll want to pay attention to this section.

The motto is: Don't SOLVE – ASK.

One of my favorite demonstrations to do in front of my speaking audiences large or small is to show them how little information I need about a person or the background scenario they are dealing with in order to coach them effectively.

Most of my coaching consists of asking

24

good questions. I demonstrate that I can help someone solve their own problem by just asking them questions.

Now remember, like I said early on, I am not asking the questions for myself to learn about the scenario or assess the situation so I can offer a solution. I am asking questions FOR the person in front me to help them problem solve on their own. The question is not for ME to understand or gather information. It's for THEM to hear themselves and work it out.

I regret to inform you that to do this you are going to have to go through "Ego-Reduction Therapy." What I mean is that you are going to have to endure not having all the answers. You'll have to stop being the problem-seeker and advice-giver. You'll have to stop being the expert. You'll have to let other people come up with their own answers. It may take longer and drive you nuts, but you are going to do it.

You'll also have to endure someone coming back to you with an idea you gave them that they now think is their own, and you'll NOT say it was yours to begin with. You will nod and encourage because only once an idea is our own do we feel motivated to take action on it. You'll have to let it be *their* idea. Can you handle this? Can you put your ego on hold and really stand in service to another person? If the answer is yes, read on.

I worked with a newly minted sales manager once who wanted, in earnest, to be an excellent manager of his team. He was eager to learn but at the same time felt that being made a leader meant having all the answers. He felt he needed to know everything to lead his team well. Despite his honest intentions to be the best he could be, his definition of what it meant to lead made him competitive and insecure. He didn't like it if he wasn't the first one with the answers, and he started losing sleep trying to anticipate every problem so he could be the one able to fix it.

When I was brought into the picture, the 'Ego-Reduction Therapy' began. Clearly, his way of leading was causing him problems. Through a series of discussions and experiments, he finally came to redefine himself as a leader and grew to embrace the idea that he could lead others by letting them work together for answers instead of providing them for everyone. The questions you are learning became his best asset.

That business example now leads me to a

big way this shows up on the home front. Allow me to appeal to the gentlemen reading this for a moment. Have you ever been told by a woman in your life that you don't listen? Have you been admonished for jumping in, trying to solve something for someone (likely a female) when that wasn't what he or she wanted? If any part of the last two questions resonated with you, then you are not alone.

How most of us listen (women, too) is that we connect what we are hearing to something we already know. It is, after all, how humans learn. We connect the new knowledge to something we can relate to, and we build from there. However, as a listener, you stop listening the minute your brain goes into looking for the connection to what you already know and how you can solve the problem.

It's likely that when you begin 'listening' your brain starts focusing on some iteration of the following:

- Is this good/bad?

- Have I heard this before?

- Why did this happen?

- How did this happen?

- Does this make sense?

- Do I agree/disagree?

- Do I like/dislike this?

- Is this right/wrong?

- Can I connect this to a past experience?

- Can I solve this?

- Do I know how to fix this?

These automatic triggers when we listen

are why we are accused of not listening!

Truly listening is important so that the right questions can be brought forth to cause change and forward motion. Good listening means helping your mind settle down so you can absorb what's being said. If you're mentally busy preparing an answer or advice, you are NOT listening. Real listening will also allow you to start reading between the lines and get a sense of what's going on beyond the words and beyond the obvious.

"Why would you want to do that?" you might ask. (There's that WHY question – always needing to understand.)

I'll tell you.

You'd want to read between the lines because you will allow the person to be heard and 'seen.' To be 'seen' means to help the other person feel understood to the point that they feel like you've penetrated the veneer we all hold up to appear capable and competent. We aren't supposed to want people to see through that wall, but when people do, we feel recognized. Once we are seen, we are more at ease and feel understood. We feel we have successfully communicated the importance of what we were trying to convey.

Again, for the gentlemen, if you help a woman feel that way, you are in her good graces.

Women, how does it feel to be understood and be able to avoid someone trying to fix something you've not asked them to fix? I can say with assurance, it feels pretty darned good. Men, you'll probably find it pretty appealing, too.

I've made a case for listening; now the questions you ask behind this momentous occasion will make you even more of a star.

CHAPTER FOUR
ASK WHAT, NOT WHY

I know it's taken a while to get to the actual questions. All that preparation was needed.

If I had just jumped to the questions, it would not have been enough. You needed to see the value in being the kind of person who would use questions as their main approach in the first place.

New questions actually come down to changing the words you choose to use in your questions. I know that sounds odd and you may become concerned whether semantics are worthy of your effort and time. Let me tell you why they are.

Different words infer different meanings and, therefore, different results in how and why you ask questions.

The conventional reason for asking questions is to gather information. We feel that to solve a problem for ourselves or to lend a solution to someone else, we need to fully understand the scenario or the situation the other person finds himself or herself in. This is only true if you are a detective or intend to offer a fix and mend the problem at the surface level.

If you're interested in true, lasting change, you may want to consider asking questions for another reason. The solution-seeker is asking questions to get to the root cause of the problem or, better yet, to help the other person (or yourself) discover his or her own solution.

When it comes to interpersonal exchanges in life or business, let's shift our perceived self-worth from the fixer/adviser and become the guide or midwife to people's brilliance. "You can feed a man a fish or you can teach him how to fish." We want the longer lasting result.

In your personal life, you'll still be a valued and trusted friend. Likely, you'll be even more so because you will help people feel good about themselves as they experience the fortitude of you reflecting their intelligence and teaching them they can trust themselves.

In business, you'll be fascinating and worth just as much money (or more) even without giving the answer. You will not compromise your status, I promise. You'll only become more valuable, and you will

lower your stress considerably as people come
to rely on you LESS! It's not a bad thing.
Get your 'juju' by being freed up to see the
bigger picture, and be a great leader rather
than being the one everyone depends on for
answers.

I'd like to introduce you to questions that
access answers, cause forward motion and
facilitate solution. I call them WISDOM
ACCESS QUESTIONS or WAQs, for short.
They do have the effect of WHACKING you
over the head and spilling out an answer.
They don't hurt, but they will make you
uncomfortable. They prod, they catch you in
the lie if there is one, and they push you out
of your comfort zone. If my clients say: " I
hate you for asking that" or "that's a good
question," I know I've done my job well.

Discomfort equals growth. That's one of

my mottos. If you're not comfortable, it's a good thing. You are being forced to grow which will ultimately be good for you despite the interim pain.

Take a look at the questions below. You'll see 'regular' questions and a bunch of WAQs. Just reading them will begin to illustrate the difference in intention and usefulness of the different questions.

Using WAQs with OURSELVES

Have you ever said:	*Ask this instead:*
Why is this happening to me?	What can I learn from this?
Why them and not me?	What can I do to get through this?
Why can't I have their luck?	What can I learn from them?
Why did I do that?	What can I do moving forward?

Using WAQs with OTHERS

Have you ever said:	*Ask this instead:*
What happened? (*tell me the juicy story*)	What happened? (*bottom line it*)
Why did you do that?	What led to that?
Did you try to fix it?	What are your options now?
Who is responsible for this?	What do we do moving forward? What will change moving forward?

You may have noticed something in common with all these Wisdom Access Questions.

They all began with WHAT.

'What' is the key to a Wisdom Access Question because it causes the specific question that has a high-yield answer. There are exceptions, however. For example: "What's wrong with you?" is not a wisdom access question. Neither is "what should I/you do?." You may also want to avoid "WHATEVER were you thinking?" And "what happens when you do/try x, y or z?" And one more to avoid is "what if you did…"

Can you see how those last two are just suggestions or advice disguised as questions? These last two I overheard just in the last month as I attempted to teach proper 'WAQing' to some 'fixer' CEOs. Clever, yes, but that's not the point.

The point is to ask better questions so you can get new results for yourself or for the person you are trying to support or direct.

If you want information then you'll be asking 'who, what, why, when and how.' If you want forward motion and solution, you'll ask WHAT?

Notice WHAT also shows up in the left column with the rest of the interrogation-like questions. The difference is the problem seeker will ask 'what' in order to understand what happened so they can assess, analyze and fix. The solution seeker will ask WHAT to peel away the layers of the problem until the solution becomes clear.

In our eagerness to understand and analyze, we tend to ask 'Why?' We want to know why something has happened. We want to explain it, understand it, be fed with knowledge so we can solve the problem or make sure we do not repeat the actions that caused the issue. However, 'why' needs to be left to scientists and inventors and drop out of our lexicon when it comes to dealing with ourselves and other people. It has no place in interpersonal communication.

Have you ever gotten a good answer to "Why did you do that?" or "Why me?" Have you? From your kids? Your direct reports? Your spouse, partner, friend? Yourself?

Case closed.

Seriously, unless it's your job to ask "Why does that cancer cell behave that way?" or "Why won't the car stop in under 30 seconds?", then you have little business using 'why' in your interpersonal exchanges and those 'conversations' you have with yourself. 'Why' is probably the worst question you could ask. It's like searching for an answer in the dark without a flashlight.

If you reflect for a moment, I'm sure you can also recall many times when using 'why' made people defensive. It has an accusatory nature to it when used to gather information about something that's gone wrong or is uncomfortable.

This brings us back to 'What'. I cannot say enough about the usefulness of questions that begin with 'What'.

Building on our problem-seeker vs. solution-seeker tendencies, the questions we ask are directly related to what our intention is behind them. Are we digging for information to solve the problem, or are we listening to the human being in front of us and trying to access the solution that serves them and the bigger picture? Are you trying to fix or are you inviting growth? Are you asking the question for you to gather knowledge, or are you asking the question to root out an organic solution or understanding for the person in front of you?

If you happen to be asking questions of yourself, are you asking them to punish yourself or to dig yourself out of the hole and onto a broader landscape?

The bottom line becomes whether you are asking the questions for YOU to understand the situation or gather information, or whether you are asking the question for the OTHER person to understand themselves and be facilitated to their own answer. When you use WHAT with yourself, you are asking the question to move yourself forward instead of keeping yourself stuck in the problem – wading in it and examining it ad nauseum.

The word WHAT has a search engine effect on the brain. The language forms a very specific question that the brain will process and return with a very specific answer. It leaves no 'wiggle room'. The direct question requires a direct answer.

The scientists at NASA that I trained to use these questions told me that for those more introverted (who think inside their head before verbalizing an answer) they really helped to draw them out. My more extroverted folks (who tend to think out loud) report that it really helps them focus and dig down to the real problem instead of talking for long periods of time with no answers becoming clear.

Using WAQs with other people will give you one of two results. One, people may feel you are too direct. The other, if they acquiesce to your inquiry, is that people will thank you for helping them think things through or bring them to a decision. If you want this new rock star status, remember you have to be the solution-seeker and not the problem-seeker and use these questions correctly.

With your new listening, you'll focus on growing the answers out of the other person through the use of your questions. It may sound like this:

- What is it costing you to do it this way?

- What do you hope to accomplish?

- What's stopping you?

- What evidence do you have that that is true?

- What are your options?

- What can you do now?

- What do you really want?

- What will get in your way?

These are of course just some examples, but look at the two question-based conversations below and compare which seems more effective.

A WAQ-LESS Questioning

Client: I'm stressing about this decision.

Coach: Why?

Client: There is a lot riding on this decision.

Coach: Which job appeals to you the most?

Client: They both have redeeming qualities. I'm just not sure what to do.

Coach: Which one appeals to you just a little more than the other?

Client: I think the one that means moving.

It would put me where I want to go.

Coach: Where is that?

Client: Doing things that would be more of a stretch would be more interesting.

Coach: Which way do you lean then?

Client: With the one that means moving.

Coach: Are you sure?

Client: No.

A WAQ-FULL Questioning

Client: I'm stressing about this decision.

Coach: What makes it so hard?

Client: Both jobs have a lot of appeal.

Coach: What are your criteria for choosing?

Client: Well, it's not just the money. One

pays less but really speaks to where I want to develop my skill set.

Coach: What other factors are weighing on you?

Client: I'm worried about how my family will adjust to a move.

Coach: What's the worst thing that could happen?

Client: That we have to come back if it doesn't work out for everyone.

Coach: What's the bottom line?

Client: I want to go for the one that's a challenge.

Coach: Great! Get the ball rolling!

Granted, I crafted these scripts, but please

know that these results and questions are based on real-time experience.

WHAT questions move things forward. The specific aspect of the question cuts through the indecision and fog that, as in the example, affects people's ability to hear and feel their own answers.

Do you have it now? WHAT questions are wisdom access questions and they produce forward motion and solution. You ask them FOR the other person, not for you. They are the questions that will train your brain to avoid problems and move to solutions. They will make you more effective in your interpersonal encounters and in your own ability to be success-minded.

To access my online list of WAQs that you can use for almost any occasion, please go to www.laurabermanfortgang.com/waq/.

You can do this. It takes practice but it is not out of your reach. Be curious. Be interested in the person coming to the answer themselves more than in trying to circumvent their work or pain by giving them an answer.

I said you'd be a rock star if you put this to work. The potential for you being a valued asset to people is high because it is thrilling for people to be shown that they have the resources to figure out their own mess. They CAN solve it. They CAN see it through and you helped them see themselves. They feel more empowered than just being handed the answer to run with.

Please take my word for it and start practicing!

CHAPTER FIVE
PICK YOUR OWN BRAIN

Once you get the hang of asking WAQs, it will be hard to use questions any other way. With that said, my experience, both personally and with clients, is that it's easier to use them with other people than it is to use them with ourselves.

Those dark times of doubt or the anxiety of searching for a solution to big problems come with a lot of emotion. As a result, your better thinking (or questions) tends to move to the backseat. It's easier and probably more familiar to stew with the pain or anxiety and seek less than healthy ways to cope. Do you eat, drink, or smoke (insert any other) when you're overwhelmed by something upsetting?

What about better questions? Talk about a harmless way to dig yourself out of a hole. It'll take practice, but it's a much better solution.

My years working with people to reframe their thinking so they are freed to take smarter actions in their life have made me aware of how the brain works. The theories I've developed, I have consulted on with highly trained psychologists and therapists to confirm what I've observed.

One of the theories behind the efficacy of the WAQs is that our brains have habits. If we are habitual worriers or negative thinkers, we have worn a very well-traveled path in the synapses of our brain. I compare those well-worn paths to riverbeds with many tributaries. When we want to get out of those well-worn paths of negativity or anxiety in our brain, we need to literally move our thinking to new pathways. I call that 'portage', the French word for carrying that is used when canoeing. If you are canoeing in a tributary of a creek or small river that then dries out or comes to an end, you have to carry your canoe (portage) to a new tributary. The same with your brain. You need to portage out of the well-worn negative path and forge a new path in your brain for solution and forward motion. The Wisdom Access Questions can help you do that.

The Wisdom Access Questions, when it comes to moving your own life forward, work very well in writing. If you're a journaler or even a pros and cons list-maker, writing down WHAT questions and then answering them for yourself can go a long way to pulling yourself out of a problem.

For example, let's assume your head is spinning because you are trying to decide whether or not to take a job in a new city. You've made your pros and cons list, you've talked to your support system, and still, you're flip-flopping on your answer and don't feel settled and sure.

Go to your computer or take out a pad of paper (some of us still like the hand to paper feel!), and try this:

- What do I want?

- What do I gain from moving?

- What do I gain from staying?

- What's the personal cost of each choice?

- What will make me proud?

- What puts me closer to my dreams?

- What's stopping me from a decision?

- What am I really afraid of?

- What else do I need in order to feel secure in the decision?

- What is the leap I need to take?

- What will success look like?

- What does my gut say?

If you answer these questions honestly, you're likely to have hit upon some fruitful answers. Some you may have already had, but now they will likely carry less emotion around them, and you'll feel more secure in them. Some of the answers may be new to you because these questions dug a little deeper.

What I can predict is that you dropped a lot of anxiety in the process of answering the

WAQs and that, if you avoid going back to the spiraling mindset, you will be able to make your decision from this new plateau. Build a support system around your choice (leave out the naysayers for now) and act.

When I was in my late twenties, I lived in New York City, pursuing an acting career and waiting on tables. (They go together, don't they?) I had hit a very rough patch in my life emotionally. OK, I had a nervous breakdown. I've written about it before in my other books. It's not a secret. My point, however, is that there was one question asked of me at that time that changed my life.

My now-husband had asked me to marry him, which precipitated the emotional break. I had made a very definitive vow in my teens that I would NEVER get married or have children, and there I was very much in love with someone who my family did not think was a suitable candidate. My internal machinations sent me over the edge. My fiancé and I had plans to go to Alaska for the summer to work at a theatre and have an adventure. I struggled with whether I should keep my commitment to go because I wasn't even sure I wanted to marry him.

I was in a downward-spiral conversation in my head. I flip-flopped on my decision hourly. I had plenty of people who would champion the side of not going and breaking up with my fiancé altogether. Finally, a very wise bartender at the restaurant I worked at got his turn to confront my mental volcano. He looked at me straight on with his swami-like bald head and white yogi uniform and asked me a WHAT question: "What does your soul say?"

I was snapped out of my hysteria and struck by that question like a dose of bitter tasting medicine that then warms and soothes your body on the way down your throat into your belly. I had the answer. I went to Alaska, and at this writing we've been married twenty one years with three kids and a pretty cool life.

I offer you that question and all the ones throughout this book to ease your way and allow you to use your greatest resource for the answers you hold: YOU. Your better part. Your higher thinker that really does know what's best for you. Using these questions is your invitation to get to know that aspect of yourself.

CHAPTER SIX
QUESTIONS FOR
CONVERSATION

Is it painful for you to go to social or business gatherings where you know few, if any, people? Many people tell me they loathe this scene and avoid it often at the cost of having an abundance of friends or business opportunities.

Equipped with great questions, you can change those gatherings into an exchange with people you don't mind at all and may even grow to like.

The key is to be very curious and use questions to connect with people. I offer you this acronym for CURIOUS.

C - Care

U - Focus on THEM; they are the U (you)

R - Reflect what the other person is saying

I - Inquire; ask questions

O - Observe your self

U - Understand before seeking to be understood (Stephen Covey)

S - Say what is true, kind, necessary and improves on the silence (Sai Baba)

C - Care: To engage with people on a meaningful level, you have to care, or at least pretend to. Seriously, being disingenuous won't get you very far. People can sense if you don't mean it or aren't truly connecting with them, and they'll move on to another conversation elsewhere. What I mean, however, is that even if you have to force yourself to care at first, do so. If you remain, curious, you'll turn that forced start into a genuine interest.

U - Focus on the other person: They are the U/you. It's about them, not YOU and your self-conscious, wish-I-wasn't-here self.

R - Reflect the other person: Show you are listening. Foster a connection and feed the conversation by repeating back to someone what they said to be sure you heard it correctly. You're not repeating what they said verbatim, but you're echoing back what you heard or any interpretation of it you may have. For example, someone might be telling me about their latest challenge at work and I might say: "It sounds like that is wearing you down." or "You're pretty upbeat for having such a big problem on your plate." I'm 'seeing' them and reflecting back what I heard and absorbed.

I - Inquire and ask questions: Here's your chance to put your WAQs to work. Keep reading to see more examples of questions you can have in your back pocket for situations just like these.

O - Observe yourself: Just notice how you are feeling once you've stepped out of your comfort zone and made a connection. If you're feeling calmer or getting a good rhythm going trying out your questions, relax into it further. Give yourself some credit and keep practicing.

U - Understand: In "The Seven Habits of Highly Effective People," the author, the late Stephen Covey, shared the principle "Seek to understand before being understood." It's a simple concept but a very powerful one, which is key to overcoming any discomfort with mingling and making conversation in less than desirable conditions. It points right back to our first "U," focusing on the other person before yourself, and "R," reflecting back what you heard. But remember, you want to avoid falling back into the habit of fixing. Care more about moving the person forward – if they are willing, of course.

S - Say what is true: Quoting a much more spiritual source, Sai Baba said: "Before you speak, ask yourself: is it kind, is it true, is it necessary and does it improve on the silence." For our purposes, let this serve as a reminder that you never know who you are speaking to, so it would serve you well to keep any negative gossip or even your own less-than-stellar opinions out of the conversation. Not easy, I know. A little humor, a quippy, snarky comment, or a ribbing of someone or the situation and you could think you are putting yourself or the other person at ease. In reality, you could end up putting your foot in your mouth and back-pedaling from here to eternity if you're not careful. So as boring as it may seem, if you're going to add to the conversation, keep it positive and gossip-free.

Now, let's get you to your questions. Your WAQs are your best date at a cocktail party or like that gregarious colleague at a business gathering. You'll want to rely on them. You'll notice I provide no pick-up lines.

Not my area of expertise.

Conversation Starters

What connection do you have to the host?

What do you think of the latest news...? (Out of corporate, or in town or whatever is appropriate?)

What do you recommend? (Referring to beverage or food selection you might be standing in front of.)

What attracted you to this group, company, or cause?

Awkward People Say Awkward Things

Other people may feel as awkward as you do or worse. In tense moments, some of us say dumb things. Instead of turning on your heels and getting the heck away from the awkward person, engage them with questions. Give them a chance to redeem themselves.

Give them the benefit of the doubt. Keep any defensive tone out of your voice, if you care to really know and make a possible connection.

What makes you say that?

What did you mean by that?

What were you hoping to accomplish by saying that? (Yes, it's forward, but you may hit on a gem by asking.)

Be Future-Oriented

What are you looking forward to for the summer, holidays, next biz quarter?

What do you see beyond that (x,y,z) problem?

What business goals are you working on right now? (Assuming you're at a biz function and it may not be appropriate early on in a conversation to ask about personal goals.)

What would success look like in this case?

What can I do to support you? What resources do you need?

What are you doing after this? (OK, I didn't say that. It was just to make sure you were still paying attention, but it is a WAQ!)

Likely, people will realize your fantastic questions have led them to talk quite a bit, and as long as they are not complete narcissists, they'll want to redirect the conversation to give you equal time. You can deflect with more WAQs but by that point, I hope you would be comfortable enough to share as well.

Armed with new conversation tools, I hope you'll attend more gatherings that can benefit you personally and professionally.

Better questions get better results, but you have to get out there!

CHAPTER SEVEN
QUESTIONS AND HAPPINESS

We've established that better questions can change your brain chemistry and put you in a more positive, forward-focused mindset and set you free from cyclical worry, fear and problems.

Can I promise that leads to happiness? I wish I could. I know the right questions can ease our mental and emotional life, which gives us more desirable outcomes, but happiness – who can really promise that?

I do believe, however, that varied degrees of increased happiness are completely in our control. I practice moving up those notches continually in my life and foster that in the people I work with or have the opportunity to reach out to through larger outlets.

What I want to leave you with as we wrap up this primer on questions is a hypothetical situation sprinkled with what I hope will become food for thought.

It's also an example of the power of questions.

When I went through my three-year bout with depression and was finally out on the other side, I saw that I only needed to know three things in order to be happy.

I had to know how to love.

I had to know peace.

And with those two, I'd probably have less trouble learning the third, which was to be happy.

None of these were givens. They were

assignments. I pass this assignment on to you as our last stop on this question-asking journey we've been on.

Imagine if you will, that you go on a journey and in your travels, you meet a powerful wizard who, unlike a genie, cannot grant you three wishes, but instead offers you three questions. He professes that if you answer these three questions with your whole heart and from the highest place of the desirable side of your dual mind (fear and love are the duality in all of us), you'll find the secret to lasting contentment, maybe even happiness.

Would you take his three questions? In case you are not sure, I offer them to you here in the first person so they can resonate in your mind and heart.

For your consideration:

What will bring me love?

What will give me peace?

What will make me happy?

What else is there? That one was mine, not the wizard's.

Will you take the wizard's questions?

* * *

You now have new tools. You can change, and even transform, yourself, your life and your business and personal relationships with Wisdom Access Questions and your new understanding of the artistry of questions.

If all else fails, get quiet, take time to hear the answer and ask: "What does my soul say?"

Somewhere in you, you have the answers.

I know it.

THE END

ABOUT THE AUTHOR

Laura's professional life is anchored by her international reputation as a pioneer in the personal coaching field. Only one expression of her twenty-two plus years of supporting people to find meaning, purpose and satisfaction in their lives, Laura is also a best-selling author, sought-after speaker, corporate spokesperson, performer and interfaith minister.

Laura's no-nonsense, entertaining writing and speaking style has helped her uplifting messages spread far and wide. She is the best-selling author of five books now published in 13 languages. They include: *The Prosperity Plan, Now What? 90 Days to a New Life Direction, Living Your Best Life, Take Yourself to the Top* and *The Little Book On Meaning*, which was a finalist for a Books for a Better Life award, alongside the Dalai Lama.

Laura has also been a media perennial for years. Her appearances on Oprah, The CBS Early Show, NBC's Today, Good Morning America, various nationally syndicated and cable outlets, as well as a long stint as contributing editor for Redbook Magazine and as a Huffington post blogger, have helped her reach millions of people who want to improve their work and life.

Through her coaching company, InterCoach, Inc./Now What?® Coaching, Laura has provided coaching to diverse clients ranging from homemakers, celebrities and Fortune 500 companies to NASA and the Army Corps of Engineers.

One of the first to be formally trained as a professional coach and hold a credential, Laura was a founding member and early board member of the International Coach Federation.

Laura holds a B.S. in Communications from Boston University, is a graduate of Coach University, and was ordained in 2006 by One Spirit Interfaith Seminary in New York City.

A wife and mother of three, Laura resides in New Jersey with her family.

To access Laura's **online list of WAQs** that you can use for almost any occassion, please go to www.laurabermanfortgang.com/waq/.

For more information on **career coaching or executive coaching**, you can visit:

www.laurabermanfortgang.com

www.nowwhatcoaching.com

Please keep me informed on how your question-asking journey progresses. I'd really like to know. *LBF*

PO Box 125, Montclair, NJ 07042

(973) 857-8180

lbf@laurabermanfortgang.com

77569696R00050

Made in the USA
Columbia, SC
23 September 2017